21st CENTURY LIVES
ACTION HEROES AND SUPERHEROES

Adam Sutherland

WAYLAND

First published in 2010 by Wayland

Wayland
338 Euston Road
London NW1 3BH

Wayland Australia
Level 17/207 Kent Street
Sydney, NSW 2000

Senior editor: Camilla Lloyd
Designer: Stephen Prosser
Picture researcher: Shelley Noronha

Picture Acknowledgments: The author and publisher would like to thank the following for allowing their pictures to be reproduced in this publication: Cover & 5: © epa/Corbis; © David Fisher/Rex Features: 1& 6; © Rex Features: 1, 16, 18; © 20thC.Fox/Everett/Rex Features:7, 17, 19; © Sara De Boer/Retna Ltd./Corbis: 8; c.Warner Br.Everett/Rex Features: 9; © Tony Gentile/Reuters/Corbis: 10; © Universal/Everett/Rex Features: 11; Shutterstock: 12, 14; © Columbia/Everett/Rex Features: 13; © Lucasfilm/Everett/Rex Features: 15; © Ken James/Bloomberg via Getty Images: 20; © Everett Collection/Rex Features: 21.

British Library Cataloguing in Publication Data:
Sutherland, Adam.
   Action heroes and superheroes. -- (21st century lives)
   1. Superhero films--Juvenile literature. 2. Superhero
   television programs--Juvenile literature. 3. Action and
   adventure films--Juvenile literature. 4. Action and
   adventure television programs--Juvenile literature.
   5. Heroes in motion pictures--Juvenile literature.
   6. Heroes on television--Juvenile literature.
   I. Title II. Series
   791.4'3652-dc22

ISBN: 978 0 7502 6204 0

Printed in China

Wayland is a division of Hachette Children's Books, an Hachette UK company.

www.hachette.co.uk

Contents

Daniel Craig

The name is Bond, James Bond

Craig is the first blond Bond and one of the most popular.

> " The question I keep asking myself is, 'Am I the good guy or just a bad guy who works for the good side?' Bond... is an assassin when you come down to it. "
>
> **Daniel Craig to *Parade* magazine in 2008**

Full name: Daniel Wroughton Craig

Date and place of birth: 2 March 1968 in Chester, England

Education: Craig moved to London at 16 to join the National Youth Theatre. After several auditions, he was accepted at the Guildhall School of Music and Drama in 1988, where he studied alongside Ewan McGregor.

Getting started: He made his screen debut in *The Power Of One* (1991), and worked in the popular BBC2 series *Our Friends In The North* (1996), before landing supporting roles in big Hollywood movies *Lara Croft: Tomb Raider* (2001) and *Road To Perdition* (2002).

Big break: Craig came to the world's attention as an action hero when he signed a five-film deal to play James Bond. Although he was a surprise choice for the role – he is the first blond Bond - *Casino Royale* (2006) earned nearly £370 million ($600 million) around the world, making it the second most successful Bond film ever.

Subsequent action movie appearances: Craig's second turn as James Bond came in *Quantum Of Solace* (2008), adapted from a short story by Bond author Ian Fleming. He has signed up for a further three Bond films.

All-round achievements: Craig was nominated for a BAFTA in 2006 for Best Actor for *Casino Royale*, and won the Best Actor award at the Evening Standard British Film Awards in 2007, both firsts for an actor playing James Bond.

Something you might not know about him: Craig is the shortest actor to play James Bond, despite being 5' 11".

Craig became the sixth actor to play James Bond in 2006's *Casino Royale*.

James Bond is the ultimate secret agent. Cunning, fearless and completely deadly, the character invented by writer Ian Fleming has made stars out of all the actors who have played him. But with the arrival of a new millennium, and competition from other action heroes like Jason Bourne, Bond was in need of modernisation. The actor chosen to reintroduce 007 to a whole new generation was British-born actor Daniel Craig.

Craig grew up in Liverpool in the 1980s, but left the recession-hit city to train as an actor in London. At the Guildhall School of Music and Drama, he studied alongside some of the UK's best known actors – Ewan McGregor, Damian Lewis and Joseph Fiennes. After graduating, Craig won supporting roles in big Hollywood films *Lara Croft: Tomb Raider* (2001) and *Road To Perdition* (2002), before landing his first leads in the crime drama *Layer Cake* (2004) and in Steven Spielberg's *Munich* (2005).

Craig became the sixth actor to play James Bond, when his appointment was announced in October 2005. He is the first blond actor to play Bond, the first to be born after the Bond films launched (*Dr No*, 1962) and the first to be born after the death of author Ian Fleming (1964). The announcement that

Craig would be the new Bond was met with surprise among the press and Bond fans worldwide. Nevertheless, four of the previous Bonds have given Craig their backing, and so have the fans. *Casino Royale* (2006) made nearly £370 million worldwide. It was the second most successful Bond film ever and won Craig a number of awards, and nominations, for his performance.

Craig is currently dating film producer Satsuki Mitchell, and has a daughter from a previous marriage. Like his Bond predecessor Pierce Brosnan, Craig is determined to play other roles apart from Bond. He has also starred as Lord Asriel in *The Golden Compass* (2007) and is soon to play Red Rackham in Steven Spielberg's *The Adventures Of Tintin: Secret Of The Unicorn* (2011). Whatever role he plays, Craig is one Bond who's always licensed to thrill!

"Daniel Craig is the greatest Bond ever and deservedly so. He was a great choice."

Pierce Brosnan speaking to Hollywood.com in 2007

Angelina Jolie
The dangerous lady

Jolie is one of the world's best-known and most photographed women.

❝I am still at heart – and always will be – just a punk kid with tattoos.❞

Angelina Jolie to Ginger Strejckek, *Season* magazine, 2005

Name: Angelina Jolie Voight

Date and place of birth: 4 June 1975 in Los Angeles, California

Education: Jolie's parents, actor Jon Voight and actress Marcheline Bertrand, split in 1976 and Jolie moved to New York with her mother and brother. At 11, the family moved back to Los Angeles and she attended Beverly Hills High School. She trained at legendary acting coach Lee Strasberg's Theatre Institute, appearing in several stage productions.

Getting started: Jolie started working as a fashion model at 14, travelling to New York and London. She took up acting seriously at 16, appearing in her brother's student films, and then finding work in Hollywood in her first film role *Cyborg 2* (1993).

Big break: Jolie won an Oscar for her role in *Girl, Interrupted* (1999) but it was the action movie *Lara Croft: Tomb Raider* (2001) that saw her reach a much bigger international audience. Playing the title role in an adaptation of the massively popular video game, she perfected her British accent and martial arts skills in a film that earned £170 million ($275 million) worldwide, and launched her reputation as a female action star.

Subsequent action movie appearances: The sequel *Lara Croft Tomb Raider: Cradle Of Life* followed in 2003. Jolie's next big action role was alongside current partner Brad Pitt in *Mr & Mrs Smith* (2005). The film earned £293 million ($478 million) worldwide, and was a big hit.

All-round achievements: Jolie became a United Nations Goodwill Ambassador in 2001, and is a tireless campaigner for refugees and displaced persons.

Something you might not know about her: As a young model, Jolie appeared in music videos for the Rolling Stones, Meat Loaf and Lenny Kravitz.

In *Wanted* (2008) Jolie trains James McAvoy to become a professional assassin.

It was this believability in her breakthrough role in *Lara Croft: Tomb Raider* (2001), the film adaptation of the huge video game franchise, that helped Jolie become probably the world's biggest female action hero. She played a cross between Indiana Jones and James Bond, and the public loved her. A new kick-ass action hero was born.

Jolie's most successful action roles to dates have come in the original *Lara Croft*, in *Mr and Mrs Smith* (2005), where she plays an assassin hired to kill her own husband, and in *Wanted* (2008), where she trains James McAvoy to be a professional hitman. Jolie and Pitt currently travel the world, sharing the parenting duties, and taking it in turns to make movies. The pair have three children of their own (Shiloh, Knox and Vivienne), and another three adopted children (Maddox, Pax and Zahara). When she's not acting, Jolie is actively involved with United Nations humanitarian work, and has spent time in Sierra Leone, Tanzania, Cambodia and other trouble spots, visiting refugee camps and using her status as a world-famous actress to publicise the plight of displaced people. She's an action hero with a heart of gold.

Angelina Jolie has always been different. She was the tomboy who travelled the world as a fashion model, the girl who left home at 14, dyed her hair purple and dreamed of being a funeral director. Now, as one half of 'Brangelina', the world's most talked-about couple with Brad Pitt, she is never far from the front pages of newspapers and magazines around the world.

Jolie is at her acting best when she puts all her experiences – emotional or physical – into her roles. She first got noticed playing a drug-addicted supermodel in *Gia* for the American TV channel HBO in 1998, and won an Oscar for her role as a psychiatric patient in *Girl, Interrupted* (1999). Few other actresses could bring menace and believability to the action roles that Jolie plays so well. When she karate kicks an opponent, fires a Magnum, dives off a waterfall, or outruns her enemies in a fast and furious car chase, you get the feeling it's something she could easily be doing in real life!

"Almost alone among leading Hollywood actresses, she is as confident slinging guns in high-tech action thrillers as she is breaking into tears in emotional dramas."

Tony Allen-Mills in *The Sunday Times*, November 2008

Christian Bale
The Dark Knight

Acting runs in the Bale family, both of Bale's grandfathers were part-time actors.

" I don't think I'm like any of the characters I've played. They're all really far from who I am. "

Christian Bale to Deadbolt.com in July 2008

Name: Christian Charles Philip Bale

Date and place of birth: 30 January 1974 in Haverfordwest, Pembrokeshire, Wales

Education: Bale is the youngest of four children, and spent his childhood in England, Portugal and the United States. His mother Jenny was a circus performer, and late father David was a commercial pilot and later Christian's manager.

Getting started: Bale made his film debut at 12, co-starring with director Steven Spielberg's then-wife Amy Irving in the TV movie *Anastasia* (1986). Irving recommended Bale to her husband, who cast him in the World War II drama *Empire Of The Sun* in 1987.

Big break: His first big budget action film was *Reign Of Fire* in 2002. The next major action role was as Batman in a relaunch of the superhero series with *Batman Begins* (2005). The film was a massive worldwide hit, taking over £230 million ($370 million).

Subsequent action movie appearances: Bale repeated his role as Batman in the sequel *The Dark Knight* (2008), alongside Heath Ledger who played the Joker. Bale next appeared in the fourth *Terminator* movie, *Terminator Salvation* (2009), as freedom fighter John Connor.

All-round achievements: Bale's role as Batman has won him several awards, including Best Hero at the 2006 MTV Movie Awards, and Favourite Superhero at the 2009 People's Choice Awards.

Something you might not know about him: His first television appearance was at 8 years old, in an advert for fabric conditioner.

A born risk-taker, Christian Bale has spent his film career mixing big budget Hollywood hits with smaller, more adventurous independent films. As a child actor, he found success in Steven Spielberg's *Empire Of The Sun* (1987), but the pressures of fame and constant attention almost caused him to give up acting before he had even started secondary school. Thankfully he was persuaded to keep acting by British actor-turned-director Kenneth Branagh, who cast him in Shakespeare's *Henry V* in 1989.

Bale has played everything from a serial killer (*American Psycho*, 1999) to a Greek fisherman (*Captain Corelli's Mandolin*, 2001). He even lost a huge 63 pounds (27kg) for *The Machinist* in 2004. Immediately after finishing filming, he won the part of Batman or Bruce Wayne in *Batman Begins* (2005) and was given six months to get into top physical shape for the part. At first he was so thin and weak that he couldn't even do one press-up, but after intensive training he put on 100 pounds (45kg). Then *Batman* director Christopher Nolan decided he was too big, and he had to lose 40 pounds (18kg)!

Batman Begins was the fifth *Batman* film, with Bale taking over from previous caped crusaders Michael Keaton, Val Kilmer and George Clooney. Bale's intense, brooding crime fighter quickly won over critics and fans who felt the earlier movies had lost their way. Bale's first *Batman* film cost £83 million and took a whopping £230 million ($370 million) at the box office. The sequel, *The Dark Knight* (2008) was even bigger. It took £97 million ($158 million) in its first weekend, £185 million ($300 million) in the first ten days, and £306 million ($500 million) in 43 days – creating three new American box office records.

Bale and director Nolan plan to work together on a new *Batman* film, but details are still top secret. What's certain is that Bale is the most successful superhero in the history of cinema.

Bale and director Christopher Nolan have made the new *Batman* movies a huge success.

"Christian is simply a great actor – something you have to have if you're going to take [the *Batman*] movies seriously."

Spider-Man director Sam Raimi about Bale to *USA Today* in 2008

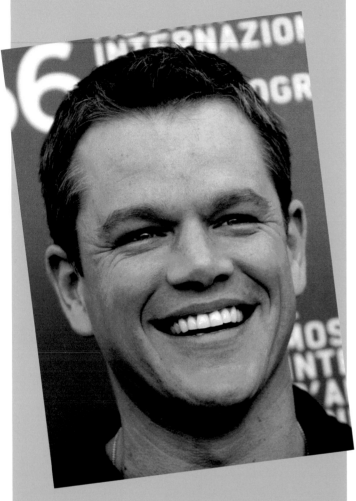

Matt Damon
The ultimate Bourne

Name: Matthew Paige Damon

Date and place of birth: 8 October 1970 in Cambridge, Massachusetts, USA

Education: Damon attended the prestigious Harvard University in Boston, Massachusetts, but dropped out before his final exams to pursue acting.

Getting started: Damon's first movie role was at 18 – one line in the Julia Roberts movie *Mystic Pizza* (1988). His first big parts were in *Geronimo: An American Legend* (1993) and *Courage Under Fire* (1996), where he played a drug-addicted Gulf War veteran.

Big break: Damon and his childhood friend Ben Affleck wrote a story about a young maths genius that became the movie *Good Will Hunting* (1997). The film was amazingly successful, receiving nine Oscar nominations. The director Steven Spielberg met Damon during filming, and cast him as the title character in the massively successful World War II action film *Saving Private Ryan* (1998).

Subsequent action movie appearances: Damon is the star of one of the greatest action movie series ever. As Jason Bourne, the trained killer with no memory, he has been incredibly popular with moviegoers around the world. The three films so far – *The Bourne Identity* (2002), *The Bourne Supremacy* (2004) and *The Bourne Ultimatum* (2007) – have made close to £615 million ($1 billion).

All-round achievements: *Good Will Hunting* earned Damon a Best Actor nomination at the Oscars, and won a Best Original Screenplay Oscar for Damon and Affleck.

Something you might not know about him: Damon has been named the best value actor in Hollywood by Forbes magazine. His films make around £18 for every 65p, or $29 for every $1, he's paid!

Damon wrote the script for Oscar-winning Good Will Hunting *while he was still at university.*

❝ Bourne is about authenticity ... Unlike Bond, you'd never see him watching a girl coming out of the sea with a bikini on. There's none of those old-fashioned macho attitudes. ❞

Matt Damon to Will Lawrence, the *Telegraph*, August 2007

Matt Damon as Jason Bourne, the trained killer who goes in search of his identity.

Damon grew up in Massachusetts and attended Harvard University, one of America's most prestigious colleges. He studied English, but already had the acting bug, and often missed lectures to attend acting auditions, or filming days on US soap *School Ties*. Eventually, juggling the two became too difficult and Damon left university in his final year to pursue acting full time. His breakthrough role was one he originally wrote with childhood friend and fellow actor Ben Affleck for an English class at Harvard. The movie *Good Will Hunting*, starring Damon as a caretaker and maths genius, was massively successful and catapulted both Damon and Affleck into the big time.

A committed campaigner for charity (along with fellow actors George Clooney and Brad Pitt he supports ONE, a campaign fighting AIDS and poverty in Third World countries), Damon is also a great actor who is 100% focused on his profession. Like one of his heroes Robert de Niro, he has earned headlines for the lengths he goes to prepare for roles. He lost 40 pounds (18kg) in just three months to play a Gulf War veteran in *Courage Under Fire* (1996) and spent six months training in martial arts, and a further six months boxing before appearing in the first *Bourne* movie.

As well as his role as Jason Bourne, Damon has starred in the *Ocean's Eleven* series of comedy-crime dramas with Clooney and Pitt, thriller *The Departed* (2006) and drama *Invictus* (2009), for which he was Oscar nominated. There is currently talk of a fourth *Bourne* movie, to be filmed in 2011. His fans can't wait to see it.

University educated, softly spoken and a typical boy-next-door, Matt Damon is not the most obvious action hero. Nevertheless, he has starred in some of the biggest box office action hits of the last ten years. *The Bourne* series of movies has made Damon a global superstar and his character, the trained killer and one-man army Jason Bourne, into a cult action hero whose influence on action films has even turned James Bond (played by Daniel Craig) into a more complex and deeper character.

"In my view [he's] the greatest movie star in the world, who's perfect for the part [of Jason Bourne] ..."

Paul Greengrass, director of *The Bourne Supremacy* and *The Bourne Ultimatum*, to www.filmstew.com 8 August, 2007

Kate Beckinsale
Vampire princess

Beckinsale is one of Britain's biggest names currently working in Hollywood.

> **" I'm a big fan of action movies. I love *Die Hard*... I don't want to be sitting on an airplane making phone calls. I want to be blowing up the elevator shaft! "**
>
> **Kate Beckinsale to IGN.com at the Toronto Film Festival, 2006**

Name: Kathryrn Bailey 'Kate' Beckinsale

Date and place of birth: 26 July 1973 in Finsbury Park, London

Education: Beckinsale went to an all-girls' school in London, where she passed A-levels in Russian, German and French. She studied French and Russian literature at New College, Oxford, but left before her final exams to pursue a full-time acting career.

Getting started: In her first year at university, Beckinsale won a part in a British movie version of Shakespeare's *Much Ado About Nothing*. The following year, she featured in two more films, and in 1995 the popular BBC drama series *Cold Comfort Farm*.

Big break: Beckinsale was determined to break into Hollywood, and in 2001 was cast as the female lead in the historical blockbuster *Pearl Harbour*. It was one of the most successful films of the year. Her first big action lead was as Selene, the vampire warrior in *Underworld* (2003).

Subsequent action movie appearances: The success of *Underworld* has led to a string of sequels, *Underworld: Evolution* (2006) and *Underworld: Rise of the Lycans* (2009). Beckinsale also played a vampire hunter alongside Hugh Jackman in *Van Helsing* (2004).

All-round achievements: Thanks to *Pearl Harbour* and the *Underworld* series, Beckinsale's films have made over £500 million ($800 million) at the box office. She has also been nominated for several MTV Movie Awards for *Underworld*.

Something you might not know about her: Beckinsale translated her script for *Van Helsing* into Russian to help with her Eastern European accent!

The role of the vampire Selene in the *Underworld* films has won Beckinsale an army of action hero fans.

Kate Beckinsale is Britain's biggest female action hero. She is the star of the hugely popular 'vampire versus werewolf' series *Underworld*, and became a household name in *Pearl Harbour*, the epic World War II drama from director Michael Bay.

Beckinsale's father, Richard, was a popular British TV actor who died of a heart attack when she was just six. She excelled at school, twice winning WH Smith Young Writers' competitions — one for short story writing, and one for poetry. She went to Oxford University to study languages, but acting was in her blood and she quickly began to win parts in some big productions. As a first year at university, she met director Kenneth Branagh, and was soon filming Shakespeare's *Much Ado About Nothing* with a cast including huge Hollywood names Denzel Washington and Keanu Reeves. She quickly landed other roles, and gave up her degree to concentrate on acting full-time.

Beckinsale could easily have followed her father's path to TV stardom. She made several high-profile UK dramas, including *Cold Comfort Farm* (1995) and Jane Austen's *Emma* (1996), but was fortunate enough to be cast as the lead female in *Pearl Harbour* (2001) when fellow actress Charlize Theron turned down the role. The film's huge worldwide success brought Beckinsale to the attention of a much larger audience.

However, it was still a surprise — not least to Beckinsale herself — to become such a successful action hero. In fact, when she was first approached to play Selene, the vampire warrior in *Underworld* (2003), she turned the part down. It was only after being persuaded to meet the director Len Wiseman (who later became her husband), and seeing the elaborate plans and drawings he had made for the film, that she was convinced to take the part.

Since then, Beckinsale has proved herself tough, fearless, acrobatic, and menacing — with just the right amount of vulnerability. She is just as believable playing a vampire as she is playing a vampire hunter!

"Occasionally Kate would pull the English rose thing but then as soon as action is said she's tougher than all of us."

Hugh Jackman, Beckinsale's co-star in *Van Helsing*, to www.ugo.com in 2004

Harrison Ford
The original action hero

Ford is entering his fourth decade in Hollywood and is still going strong!

"I don't do stunts – I do running, jumping and falling down. After 25 years I know exactly what I'm doing."

Harrison Ford to the
Sunday Morning Herald
in October 2000

Name: Harrison Ford

Date and place of birth: 13 July 1942 in Chicago, Illinois

Education: Ford attended Ripon College in Wisconsin and became fascinated with acting after taking a drama class in his junior year.

Getting started: In 1964 he moved to California and became a 'contract actor' for Columbia Pictures. This involved playing 'bit' parts – often non-speaking and uncredited roles – in the company's films.

Big break: Film director George Lucas gave him a role in the film *American Graffiti* (1973). He then hired Ford to read lines for actors casting for *Star Wars* (1977). Ford was so impressive reading the script that Lucas cast him as Han Solo in the film. *Star Wars* became the most successful film in history, and made Ford a superstar!

Subsequent action movie appearances: Two *Star Wars* sequels followed, *The Empire Strikes Back* (1980) and *Return Of The Jedi* (1983). As well as the *Stars Wars* movies, Ford was also the star of the hugely successful *Indiana Jones* films, *Raiders Of The Lost Ark* (1981), *Indiana Jones And The Temple Of Doom* (1984) and *Indiana Jones And The Last Crusade* (1989).

All-round achievements: Ford is the most successful actor in history. His films have taken over £3.4 billion ($5.5 billion) around the world and he is the only actor to have made over £60 million ($100 million) for each decade that he's worked.

Something you might not know about him: Ford got the trademark scar on his chin at 20 when he crashed his car into a lamp-post, while trying to fasten his seat belt.

Harrison Ford is probably the biggest action movie star in history. He has played two iconic, unforgettable action heroes – Han Solo and Indiana Jones – and topped box office takings in the 1970s, 1980s and 1990s. Not bad for someone who almost gave up acting to become a full-time carpenter.

Ford grew up in Illinois, but dropped out of college to move to Los Angeles. His ambition was to work in radio, but he eventually signed a £90 ($150) per week contract to play small parts for Columbia Pictures. The money was low, so Ford made ends meet by working as a self-taught carpenter. He built stage sets for rock band The Doors, cabinets for director George Lucas, and even an office for *The Godfather* director Francis Ford Coppola.

These industry connections finally started to pay off. George Lucas cast Ford in his 1950s-themed drama *American Graffiti*, and then hired him to provide support to actors casting for *Star Wars*. The story is that Lucas didn't find anyone who could do the job as well as Ford, so he hired him to play Han Solo. Ford's films during the 1980s and 1990s were huge. As well as the *Star Wars* and *Indiana Jones* films, he also starred in the science fiction classic *Blade Runner* (1982), the action thriller *Frantic* (1988) and the Tom Clancy CIA films *Patriot Games* (1992) and *Clear And Present Danger* (1994).

A late starter as a leading man (Ford was 35 when he played Han Solo in *Star Wars*), his career has now spanned over three decades. Ford has taken a few breaks from acting to spend time with his fiancée, the actress Calista Flockhart, and her adopted son Liam, but he's not planning on retiring just yet. Most recently, he made the fourth *Indiana Jones* film, *Indiana Jones And The Kingdom Of The Crystal Skull* (2008), which was another great box office success. There are even plans for a fifth film. Who would have guessed there would be a 70-year-old Indiana Jones?

The fedora (a type of hat) worn by Ford in the *Indiana Jones* films is now on display at the Smithsonian Institute in Washington.

"[Harrison Ford] is best known as being the hero. That's what he's good at, mixing ordinariness... with luck and strength that comes out of nowhere. The winner against the odds."

Chrissy Iley in the *Observer*, 27 April 2008

A talented singer and dancer, Jackman has won several Tony and Emmy awards for his performances.

❝ When I was 28, I was at the National Theatre in London doing a production of *Oklahoma!* And that was about as far as I ever dreamed I'd go. Everything since then has been a little surreal and there's not a day that goes by where I don't thank my lucky stars. ❞

Hugh Jackman to The CinemaSource.com, 2009

Name: Hugh Michael Jackman

Date and place of birth: 12 October 1968 in Sydney, Australia

Education: Attended the all-boys Knox Grammar School in Sydney, and became school captain in 1986. Jackman went on to earn a degree in Communications at the Sydney University of Technology, graduating in 1991. After university, he completed a one-year acting course at the Actors' Centre in Sydney before attending the Western Australia Academy of Performing Arts (WAAPA), graduating in 1994.

Getting started: Jackman's early film roles include the Australian drama *Erskineville Kings* (1999) and the romantic comedy *Paperback Hero* (1999).

Big break: In 2000, he was cast as Wolverine in director Bryan Singer's *X-Men*. The film earned £160 million ($300 million) worldwide, and turned Jackman into an instant action movie hero.

Subsequent action movie appearances: Jackman has starred in three more *X-Men* films so far, *X2 – X-Men United* (2003), *X-Men: The Last Stand* (2006) and *X-Men Origins: Wolverine* (2009). He also played a vampire hunter in *Van Helsing* (2004).

All-round achievements: Not only is Jackman a movie superhero, he's also an excellent singer and dancer. He first became known outside Australia playing the lead in the musical *Oklahoma!* in London's West End, for which he earned an Olivier Award nomination for Best Actor in a Musical. In 2004 he won a Tony Award for another musical, *The Boy From Oz*.

Something you might not know about him: At 6' 3", Jackman is a foot taller than the Wolverine comic book character. He was often shot at unusual angles, and his co-stars wore platform soles to make him look smaller!

When Jackman was originally offered the part of Wolverine, his wife advised him to turn it down. She's happy now that he ignored her!

Hugh Jackman has an amazing range of talents. Not only has he become famous around the world playing the indestructible superhero Wolverine in the *X-Men* series of films, he is also an award-winning singer and dancer who has starred in musicals from Broadway in New York to London's West End. And if that's not enough, he also hosts award ceremonies, including the 2009 Oscars (with jokes supplied by *The Office's* Ricky Gervais), and the Tony Awards from 2003-2005. He has even won an Emmy Award for hosting the Tonys!

Jackman's first big career turning point came in 1992, when he turned down a role in Australian soap *Neighbours* to pursue his acting studies. Then a big slice of luck came his way when actor Dougray Scott, who was supposed to be playing Wolverine in the first *X-Men* film (2000), had to pull out of the role when the film he was working on overran by two months.

Jackman accepted the role and became everyone's favourite mutant. His high rise hair, huge sideburns, and metal claws have become instantly recognisable trademarks, and have helped the films make over £900 million ($1.5 billion) at box offices around the world. *Wolverine* has already had his own spin-off movie, *X-Men Origins: Wolverine* (2009), with a follow-up planned.

Jackman was rumoured to have been shortlisted for the role of James Bond (later given to Daniel Craig, pages 4-5), but when he's not fighting evil as Wolverine, he tends to stay away from action roles, and is more often found in historical dramas like director Baz Luhrmann's *Australia* (2008) or musical adaptations like the rumoured remakes of *Carousel* and *Sunset Boulevard*. He has provided voiceovers for two animated movies, *Happy Feet* and *Flushed Away* (both 2006). He is a singing and dancing mutant!

"Jackman has a particular affinity for Wolverine ... because it was the character that gave him his start in Hollywood. [His] performance won over both general audiences and fans of the cult hit comic book."

John Hiscock, the *Daily Telegraph*, 30 April 2009

Will Smith

Hollywood's favourite action hero

Smith is the only actor in history to have eight consecutive films open at Number 1 at the US box office.

" I consider myself to be of basically average talent. What I have that other people don't have is an obsessive, raw animal drive [to succeed] ... "

Will Smith to *Readers' Digest*, December 2006

Name: Willard Christopher 'Will' Smith Junior

Date and place of birth: 25 September 1968 in West Philadelphia

Education: Smith attended Overbrook High School in Philadelphia, where his ability to charm his way out of trouble earned him the nickname 'Prince'. He started rapping in his teens, and teamed up with school friend Jeff Townes to become DJ Jazzy Jeff and the Fresh Prince. The pair had huge chart success, even winning a Grammy (the equivalent of a musical Oscar).

Getting started: Smith's first acting experience came in the Number 1 US TV comedy *The Fresh Prince Of Bel-Air*, which ran for six series from 1990-1996. Smith basically played himself – a street-smart West Philadelphia kid who ends up living in Beverly Hills. The show's success launched his film acting career.

Big break: The action comedy *Bad Boys* (1995) established Smith as a bankable star, and his next two films *Independence Day* (1996) and *Men In Black* (1997) were hugely successful summer blockbusters.

Subsequent action movie appearances: Smith has had a great run of action movie hits, including *Enemy Of The State* (1998), *Men In Black II* (2002), *I, Robot* (2004), *I Am Legend* (2007) and *Hancock* (2008).

All-round achievements: Smith won the first ever Grammy for a rap record for the song *Parents Just Don't Understand*. He has also been nominated for two Oscars, for his portrayal of boxer Muhammad Ali in *Ali* (2001), and *The Pursuit Of Happyness* (2006).

Something you might not know about him: Smith is the only actor in history to have eight consecutive films earn more than £60 million ($100 million) at the US box office.

Smith as Detective Del Spooner in 2004's *I, Robot*. The story was based on a collection of short stories by sci-fi writer Isaac Asimov.

Charming, funny, hard-working and multi-talented, Will Smith has been successful at everything he has turned his hand to. The chart-topping rapper, TV star and movie action hero has been nominated for two Oscars, four Golden Globes, has won several musical Grammys and has had two multi-platinum albums, *Big Willie Style* (1997) and *Willennium* (1999). He is also the only leading actor to have eight consecutive films open at No 1 at the US box office.

Smith's musical career made him a millionaire by the time he was 20, but he got in trouble with the US tax office, who found him owing £1.75 million ($2.8 million) in unpaid taxes, leaving him nearly bankrupt. His big acting break came when he met music producer and manager Benny Medina who was writing a TV comedy about his own life. The pair hit it off and Smith was chosen to play the title character in *The Fresh Prince Of Bel-Air*. The show's worldwide success launched Smith's acting career, which was built on a series of bigger and better summer blockbusters, from *Bad Boys* (1995) to *Men In Black* (1999) and more. Smith's broad public appeal across all ages, men and women, black and white gives him the rare quality of being able to 'open' a film. In other words he guarantees success at the box office.

The actor's popularity has even spread as far as the White House. President Barack Obama has said that if a film is ever made about his life, he would like Will Smith to play the part because "he has the ears"!

Smith is married to actress Jada Pinkett Smith. The couple have two children, Jaden (Smith's co-star in *The Pursuit Of Happyness*) and Willow (who appears as his daughter in *I Am Legend*). Notoriously hard working, Smith once held the world record for most premieres attended, when he appeared on three red carpets – in Manchester, Birmingham and then London – within 12 hours for the film *Hitch* in 2005.

"[Will Smith] has consistently delivered hits, most often as a good-natured guy saving the rest of us from the trauma of aliens, robots, crooks or poor dating habits."

Rebecca Winters Keegan, *Time Magazine*, November 2007

Arnold Schwarzenegger
The Terminator

Schwarzenegger was first elected Governor of California in 2003.

❝Strength does not come from winning. Your struggles develop your strengths. When you go through hardships and decide not to surrender, that is strength.❞

Arnold Schwarzenegger on *The Tonight Show with Jay Leno*, 2008

Name: Arnold Alois Schwarzenegger

Date and place of birth: 30 July 1947 in Thal, Styria, Austria

Education: Schwarzenegger was a keen sportsman at school, but at 14 he gave up everything to concentrate on bodybuilding. The sport was virtually unheard of at the time. He started an intensive training regime and by 18 won his first major title, Junior Mr Europe.

Getting started: Schwarzenegger won the first of his five Mr Universe titles in 1967, and moved to America the following year. He continued bodybuilding, but also trained hard as an actor. His first big film role was playing Hercules in *Hercules In New York* (1970). He was also the star of the bodybuilding film *Pumping Iron* in 1977.

Big break: His first box office hit was the fantasy action film *Conan The Barbarian* in 1982. This was followed by a sequel *Conan The Destroyer* in 1984. The same year, Schwarzenegger made his first appearance as the legendary cyborg (half man, half robot) in director James Cameron's *The Terminator*. The film made him a superstar.

Subsequent action movie appearances: The Austrian actor had a great run of action hits, including *Commando* (1985), *The Running Man* (1987), *Predator* (1987), *Total Recall* (1990), and *Terminator 2: Judgement Day* (1991). *Terminator 2* was the highest-grossing film of the year.

All-round achievements: Schwarzenegger is currently serving as the 38th Governor of California. He was first elected in October 2003, and re-elected in November 2006.

Something you might not know about him: His nickname is 'the Governator', a combination of Governor and Terminator.

The Terminator, directed by *Avatar*'s James Cameron, made Schwarzenegger a star around the world.

Arnold Schwarzenegger is a great American success story. Born in a tiny Austrian village, he set – and achieved – a series of almost unbelievable goals for himself and has become famous around the world.

First of all, he popularised and conquered the world of bodybuilding, starting with Junior Mr Europe in 1965. At the time, he was serving in the Austrian army, and went AWOL (absent without leave) during training to take part in the contest. On his return, he spent a week in an army jail as punishment. He won the first of five Mr Universe titles in 1967, and moved to the United States the following year. He combined his bodybuilding with dialect classes, and his second great goal – acting lessons. He made his first film in 1970, *Hercules In New York*, under the name Arnold Strong. Unfortunately, his accent was so strong and difficult to understand that another actor spoke his lines in the finished version of the film.

Nevertheless, Schwarzenegger kept working hard and made his breakthrough film, *Conan The Barbarian*, in 1982. Two years later, he starred in his most memorable role – the killer cyborg in *Terminator* (1984). Thanks to a series of big budget, action-packed roles, he became one of America's best-loved action heroes, making two further *Terminator* films,

Terminator 2: Judgement Day (1991) and *Terminator 3: Rise Of The Machines* (2003), and other box office action hits including *Last Action Hero* (1993), *True Lies* (1994), *Eraser* (1996) and *Batman & Robin* (1997).

He was always able to make fun of his tough guy image and also made a string of very popular comedies with director Ivan Reitman: *Twins* (1998), *Kindergarten Cop* (1990) and *Junior* (1994). In 2003, Schwarzenegger announced he was running for political office, and in October of the same year he achieved his third great goal, being elected Governor of California. Now in his second term as Governor, Schwarzenegger combines the common sense of a life-long politician with the charisma of a movie star. The perfect Governor for Hollywood!

"Schwarzenegger is the most famous immigrant in America. He overcame a thick Austrian accent and transcended the unlikely background of body building to become the biggest movie star in the world in the 1990s"

LA Weekly, 2002

Halle Berry

Halle Maria Berry (born August 14, 1966 in Cleveland, Ohio) is Hollywood's most recognisable African-American actress. An Oscar-winner for her role in *Monster's Ball* (2001), Berry has also starred in a string of hit action films, most notably *X-Men* (2000), where she plays the superhero Storm, and its sequels *X2 – X-Men United* (2003) and *X-Men: The Last Stand* (2006). She played Catwoman in the 2004 film, and has even starred as a Bond girl in 2002's *Die Another Day*.

Berry is one of the highest-paid actresses in Hollywood, earning over £6 million ($10 million) per film. She was named after Halle's Department Store, a local landmark in Cleveland, and was the first African-American entrant in Miss World, finishing sixth in 1986. In the late 1980s, Berry began to pursue an acting career, getting her first big break in the 1991 hit *Jungle Fever*. The huge success of *X-Men*, which took £180 million ($300 million) around the world, helped turn her into an action movie superstar.

Bruce Willis

Walter Bruce Willis was born 19 March 1955 in Idar-Oberstein, West Germany to a German mother and a US soldier father. Bruce's father left the army in 1957 and moved the family to Penns Grove, New Jersey where Bruce went to the local high school and struggled with a stutter. However, he found that when he was on stage, his stutter disappeared, and so he began attending the school's drama club. After a series of part-time jobs ranging from security guard to private investigator, Bruce decided to concentrate on acting.

The US public knew Bruce as a wise-cracking detective in the TV series *Moonlighting* (1985-89), but his role in the movie *Die Hard* (1988)

shot him to action hero fame. The film made close to £85 million ($140 million) worldwide, and turned Bruce into an action hero icon. He went on to make three more *Die Hard* films, *Die Hard 2* (1990), *Die Hard With A Vengeance* (1995) and *Live Free Or Die Hard* (2007). He also starred in Quentin Tarantino's *Pulp Fiction* (1994), *Hostage* (2005), *Lucky Number Slevin* (2006) and *16 Blocks* (2006). His films have made over £1.5 billion ($2.5 billion) in the US alone.

Shia LaBeouf

Shia LaBeouf is one of Hollywood's new generation of leading men. Born Shia Saide LaBeouf on 11 June 1986 in Los Angeles, California, the young actor is already the star of two *Transformers* films, and has played Harrison Ford's young sidekick in the most recent *Indiana Jones* film, *Indiana Jones And The Kingdom Of The Crystal Skull* (2008). The son of a Vietnam war veteran and a hippy ex-ballerina, LaBeouf spent much of his childhood on the streets of LA, as part of his parents' street performance group. He took up acting seriously at 12, and appeared in several TV series, including *The X-Files*, and *Even Stevens* for the Disney Channel.

His big break came in the Disney movie *Holes*, which also featured Jon Voight (Angelina Jolie's father). Director Steven Spielberg was a big fan of LaBeouf's performance in the film, comparing him to a young Tom Hanks, and has cast him in three films that he either directed or produced – *Transformers: The Game* (2007), *Indiana Jones* (2008) and the thriller *Eagle Eye* (2008). LaBeouf was in the second *Transformers* film entitled *Revenge of the Fallen* in 2009 with popular co-star Megan Fox. It is thought that a third *Transformers* film will be released in 2011.

Sylvester Stallone

Sylvester Gardenzio 'Sly' Stallone (born 6 July 1946 in New York City) was one of the world's biggest action movie stars. Two of his characters, soldier John Rambo, and boxer Rocky Balboa, became household names and their films earned hundreds of millions of dollars at the box office. Just as impressive, Stallone overcame slurred speech and a partially paralysed face (caused by a severed nerve at birth) to make it as a Hollywood leading man.

Stallone wrote the screenplay for *Rocky* (1976) in just three days after being inspired by a Muhammad Ali boxing match. The film was nominated for ten Oscars, and won Best Picture and Best Director. In total, Stallone has starred in four *Rambo* films, and written and starred in six *Rocky* films, the most recent being *Rocky Balboa* (2006).

Other career highlights include *Nighthawks* (1981), *Cliffhanger* (1993), *Demolition Man* (1993), comic book adaptation *Judge Dread* (1995) and *Spy Kids 3-D: Game Over* (2003). Stallone is now rumoured to be working on *Rocky 6*!

Tobey Maguire

Tobias Vincent 'Tobey' Maguire (born 27 June 1975 in Santa Monica, California) is an unlikely superhero. Looking more like a librarian than a bodybuilder, he nevertheless shot to superstardom playing the web-spinning Spider-Man. He acted alongside Kirsten Dunst as his love interest, in the series of hit movies *Spider-Man* (2002), *Spider-Man 2* (2004) and *Spider-Man 3* (2007).

Maguire dropped out of high school and wanted to be a chef until his mother offered him £60 ($100) to take a drama course. He started working as a child actor in Hollywood, and made his first appearance in a film called *The Wizard* (1989).

Maguire played a teenager well into his mid-20s, getting his big break in *The Ice Storm* (1997), which led to other major roles in *The Cider House Rules* (1999) and *Wonder Boys* (2000). In September 2008, *The Sunday Times* reported that Maguire had signed a £30 million ($50 million) contract to make *Spider-Man 4* and *Spider-Man 5*. *Spider-Man 4* started filming in 2010, and is due for release in May 2011.

Tom Cruise

Thomas Cruise Mapother IV was born on 3 July 1962 in Syracuse, New York. He won a scholarship to a church school and had plans to become a Catholic priest, but he also loved sports, playing American football and hockey. When a knee injury kept him out of the high school wrestling team, Cruise successfully auditioned for the lead role in the school musical and was bitten by the acting bug.

Cruise got his big break in the box office hit *Risky Business* (1983), where he danced in his underwear, miming to a rock 'n' roll song! His first big action hit was the fighter pilot drama *Top Gun*, which became the highest grossing film of 1986. He also starred as a racing driver in *Days Of Thunder* (1990).

In 1996, Cruise made the first of three *Mission: Impossible* movies. *Mission: Impossible II* followed in 2000, and *Mission: Impossible III* in 2006. The remake of the 1960s TV series has earned over £600 million ($1 billion) around the world. *Mission Impossible IV* will be the next, and possibly final installment, in the *Mission Impossible* series.

Cruise gave a heroic performance in *The Last Samurai* (2003), and played the lead in *War of the Worlds* in 2005. The action-comedy, *Knight and Day*, starring Cruise and Cameron Diaz was released in 2010.

Cruise married Nicole Kidman in 1990, they divorced nearly ten years later and have two adopted children together. In 2006, Cruise married Katie Holmes and they have one

Index

21st Century Lives

Contents of books in the series: